WHEN MAN LISTENS

WHEN MAN LISTENS

BY

CECIL ROSE

When man listens, God speaks;
When man obeys, God works.

NEW YORK
OXFORD UNIVERSITY PRESS
1937
2nd Pri   ig 1938

Originally published by Oxford Univeristy Press, December 1937
Republished by Healing-Hal   m Tuchy Palmieri
BookSurge Publisning 2008

To

THE OXFORD GROUP

THE GROWING ARMY OF MEN AND WOMEN
WHO ARE PROVING AFRESH FOR OUR GENERATION
THAT

When man listens, God speaks;
When man obeys, God works.

CONTENTS

THE chapters of this book are an attempt to set down briefly the simple elements of Christian living. I believe that there is nothing in them which cannot be found in the New Testament. It is my unpayable debt to my friends of the Oxford Group that they brought me face to face with the challenge of this way of life, and with patience, frankness, and love are showing me how to find and live it more fully.

Meeting the Group has meant for me not only a new release and power in my own life, but the birth in me of a new hope for the world. Ideals which seemed to recede further with every year, are being brought within reach through men and women who have faced such a personal revolution that God is, through them, bringing about a revolution in society.

This book is itself a product of the team work to which the Oxford Group is lending fresh and deeper meaning. Without the first suggestion of one friend and the later help of a good many others, it could not have reached its present form. For what has been written I must myself take full responsibility. For their help I gladly acknowledge my debt.

CECIL ROSE.

HOYLAKE,
   December, 1936.

I

GOD IN CONTROL

WHEN a forty horse-power car refuses to climb a hill, it is time to find out what is wrong. Had it been a car of eight horse-power, or even ten horse-power, we might have concluded that the hill was too steep, but a forty horse-power car is made to climb any hill.

We are in the same plight to-day with religion. It looks as though Christianity had stopped on the hill. Certainly the type of Christianity to which we have been most accustomed has not been able to surmount the hatreds and fears which make war, or the selfishness which results in want amidst a world of plenty. It has also failed to reach the need of vast numbers of men and women who are at war with themselves and in great want of peace, freedom from fear, and the power to deal with life victoriously.

To plead the difficulties of the time—war reactions, anti-religious tendencies, and the rest—is to beg the question. The power which Christians claim to wield is God's power. That should be enough to take us up any hill and over all obstacles.

Why has it not done so?

If we choose, we may say that the car is a fraud, that it was never capable of a quarter of its alleged horse-power, and we may leave it at the roadside. That will not take us up the hill. And we do need desperately some means of getting to the top. For one thing the gradient is dangerous. We are in

14

danger of running backwards at any moment into social chaos, or personal unhappiness and defeat. But apart from danger, there is in us the desire for life at a level of freedom, effectiveness, and happiness greater than anything we have yet reached. We need something to lift us to this level. We should be silly to abandon the car before we have made quite sure that its breakdown is not our fault and that it cannot be put right.

There is all the more reason to examine our car, since there is none other available. It is not only our type of religion which seems to have failed: education has not overcome the passions which make war, nor has it emptied the divorce courts. Statesmanship is baulked and helpless in a fear-ridden world that cannot outlive its memories. Industry and commerce have built up the marvellous and intricate mechanism of production and distribution, but they have not been able to make it proof against the grit that men are throwing so plentifully into the wheels. Science has provided us with amazingly varied means for the enrichment of life, but it has not given us happiness. Where is the alternative to another trial of the Christian solution?

Besides, the Christian solution is giving more signs of working than perhaps we thought. When an ex-communist and a Russian princess speak on the same platform of the answer that Christ has brought to their hatred, we may well ask how it happened, and whether it cannot happen again to others. When the wife of a Blue-shirt officer in Ireland discovers how to work for a new Ireland in friendship

with a woman who wheeled her baby through Dublin streets in a perambulator half-full of Mills' bombs, we begin to see a possible end to civil strife. When the home of two people, who were on the edge of divorce, becomes a centre of Christian action, we know that there is a real working answer to unhappy marriages. And when this same answer begins to work out, as it is doing to-day, in the lives of thousands of men and women, giving them release from all manner of personal problems, not only is it worth while, but it is imperative, that we should find out whether it can work on such a scale that it can remake a nation—and a world.

Perhaps we had the brakes on all the time, or perhaps we had allowed dirt to block the petrol-pipe.

If we are to try out the Christian life, we must understand what it is.

There is a widespread notion that a Christian is a man who tries to live up to certain ideals. That is to miss the most important fact about him. A Christian is not a man who is trying to *do* something. He is a man who has *received* something. He is a man raised to a new level of power. This is evident as soon as we turn to the New Testament.

The New Testament contains something far greater than a new set of ideals. It is the story of what God can do with men and women when they let Him—the revolution that takes place when God is given control of lives. The people we meet in the Acts of the Apostles are clearly men and women to whom something has happened. They are acting

with a courage that was not theirs at first. They speak with a force and clarity not natural to their uncultured tongues. They have shed the self-seeking and contentious spirit that marred their earlier record. They are irrepressible in their confidence and joy, when, before, they were so easily daunted. For the most part they are obscure folk, yet they succeed in turning their world upside down. Here are personalities released and raised to a new level of effectiveness. They are adequate in a new way to meet all demands.

That is what all of us want to be.

We may be looking for the secret in all sorts of places where it cannot be found, but the object of our quest is *adequacy for life*. That is exactly what Jesus promised. He did not say, 'I have come that you might have a new and more exacting set of rules,' or 'I have come to call you to strive after a higher level of conduct.' He said, 'I have come that you might have *Life*—and have it to the full.' 'Life to the full' must mean a life set free from the haunting sense of failure, victorious over temptation, released from fears, with a new mastery over moods, impulses, and habits, a clear purpose, and a power which makes possible the effective use of the whole personality. If that sounds a sweeping programme, it is no more than is promised in the New Testament. A body of people who had found this secret could change the world.

How is it to be found?

Jesus announced His answer to man's need in one phrase, '*the Kingdom of God*'—that is the Kingship of

God—God's complete control of life, of your life and mine.

What we see happening to men and women in the Acts of the Apostles is what happens when God is really allowed to take over and run our lives Himself. Our fundamental need is for Him to be in charge. Our fundamental sin is that we have not allowed Him to be. We may have referred some of our difficulties and questions to Him. We may have accepted portions of His programme for us—selected according to taste—but we have not given Him complete command. The self-run life has been our trouble.

Peace, direction, power—the fullness of life—await the complete surrender of ourselves to God for His purposes. This is the great experiment that is waiting to be made—giving God control.

How do we begin the experiment?

To put it very simply, God cannot take over my life unless I am *willing*. Willingness is not a matter of feeling. It is not a vague desire that God should change me. It is not an impulsive resolve to obey God in future. It is a very practical thing.

If a man is bankrupt and consents to his chief creditor reorganizing and running the business, the first thing he must do is to produce the books—all of them. The difficulty with so many debtors is that they conceal some of their debts, or fail to mention some particularly foolish blunder or some doubtful transaction to which fear prompted them. A satisfactory re-organization is impossible if there is only a partial disclosure. If, then, I want God to take

control of my life, the first thing I must do is to produce the books. I must be willing to look with God at everything I know about myself, and at everything He can show me when I honestly test my life by what I see of His will in Christ.

A good way to begin this examination of the books is to test my life beside the Sermon on the Mount. A convenient and pointed summary of its teaching has been made under four heads—Absolute Honesty, Absolute Purity, Absolute Unselfishness, and Absolute Love.

It is very necessary to keep that word 'Absolute' in mind. It is like a clear white light searching into all sorts of hidden corners. It makes sure that I shall not overlook the places where I was content with a second best or excused myself for a compromise.

Honesty? Well, that is not too bad. I do not rob the till, or make fraudulent returns to the Inspector of Taxes. (Or do I?) But *Absolute* Honesty? That looks different. Do I make elaborate excuses over something that I have simply forgotten to do? Do I waste my employer's time by lateness or slackness? Am I living in the open with my family?

Absolute Purity? What would my thought-life look like on the screen?

Absolute Unselfishness? Why do I get touchy and defensive when people criticize me? Am I only thinking of them, or is it my own feelings and reputation for which I still care? And what would my family say about my *absolute* unselfishness?

Absolute Love? Yes, I know that I did not begin the trouble, and as far as I know, have done nothing

24

to keep it going, but what have I done to end it? And what about my likes and dislikes?

It may be useful at this point if I get a pencil and paper, and make some notes. This business of looking into the books is taking me further than I expected, but I must see it through.

My life is many-sided. How far am I allowing God to take control over its various interests and activities? There is my business. Is He managing director? There is my money. Does He spend it? My time. Does He dispose of it? There are my friendships, my home, my career, my leisure. How far is God in absolute control of these? Willingness for Him to take charge will mean an honest and thorough scrutiny of every area of my life. It will bring to light all sorts of things that I have not been willing for God to alter—habits, indulgences, wrong relationships, personal ambition, opinions, and sheer self-will. Sin will take on a deeper meaning for me. Anything that I am not willing to submit to God is sin.

The next practical result of my 'willingness' will be that I shall take any steps which God shows me, to put right the wrong I have done. There may be a broken relationship to be healed, an apology to be offered, a sin to be confessed to the person most concerned, reparation to be made for some dishonesty. For one man the step of honesty with God and with his fellows meant offering to go back to the country he had left and face his trial for breach of trust. For another it meant admitting to his University that he had received a diploma on the

basis of a false statement. Others have had to disillusion altogether misled families about the kind of persons they really are.

These first steps of restitution are absolutely necessary if I am to start the new life clear with God and other people. There will be a great many things I can never put right now. Even the restitution I can make will seem altogether inadequate. I must simply accept the wonder of God's forgiveness, but I dare not take it unless I am prepared to do everything which can honestly and usefully be done to put wrong right.

I must be just as practical in making effective the new quality of life that God is leading me to see. If I realize my indiscipline, I must pin myself down to some definite step—perhaps getting up earlier, replying to letters, or promptness in keeping my appointments. If I find myself tied up by shyness, it may mean going out among people, or speaking in front of them until the fear is broken. If God speaks to me about unselfishness, it may involve some simple, but costly step at home. If my treatment of my employees, or my attitude to my business rivals has been unloving, there will be immediate steps to take in establishing new relationships. Vague resolutions and dreams of what I might be, never lead to God-control. I must let God pin me down to the next thing to be done.

These, then, are the first elements in a surrender of life to God—honest and thorough facing of myself with God, restitution to others, and practical steps of new obedience. They are best talked through with another person. It is so easy to deceive myself, to

escape the real shame and humiliation of sin, or to evade the necessary steps. To face a completely honest talk with someone I can trust makes me see myself as I could never do in any other way. It may bring to light much that I have missed. It will certainly make it harder for me to go back or postpone carrying out my resolutions. This is one of the purposes for which God has given us fellowship. It is dangerous to neglect it.

Surrender goes on. It is not simply an initial act. It is a process carried deeper every day. We find out more of ourselves to give to God. We find out more of what God can do with us. But it must *begin*, and it is possible for us now to give all we know of ourselves to all we know of God.

This initial surrender, if it is thorough and honest, is met at once from God's side. When we hand over, God takes charge, and things begin to happen. A world of strain falls from us. The business of running life is off our hands. We find that we get through more work, because it is being ordered better. We meet people we were afraid of, and discover that fear has gone. A habit that always beat us seems to have lost its power. Someone we could not bear appears to us in a new light, and we love them. We come through an ordeal and know that it was not in our own strength.

The fascinating experience of getting 're-made' has begun. The interest grows, because the process does not end with us. Other people notice the difference, and God begins to work in them. An area of life around us begins to change.

But how are we to be sure that this will happen? We want good reasons before we take such a plunge.

There is only one way to be sure—by trying. That is true of all life. It is a tremendous experiment. We only know how the water can bear us up when we get our feet off the bottom. We only find what marriage is like by getting married. We test a remedy by taking it. That is what *faith* means. It does not mean being quite confident beforehand—working up one's feelings into a state of certainty. It means making the experiment.

There are grounds for the venture. First of all, our need. Life as we have run it ourselves, has not been the kind of success of which we can be proud. It is worth while giving God the chance to run it better. Then there is all that other people say they have found. We take big steps in life on far less recommendation than is available for this step. Beyond all, there is Christ Himself. He lived this life. He lived it on the basis of absolute obedience to and trust in God. He invited us to make the experiment and prove the willingness of God.

We have to start from the place where we happen to be. Sometimes all that we can say, is, 'O God, if there is a God, take charge of my life.' If we mean it, God does take control.

II

LEARNING GOD'S PLAN

God *has a plan*. That is one of the great affirmations of the Christian Faith.

In that plan each of us has a part. All the world's troubles and all our own troubles arise from our failure to discover that plan and our part in it. God's plan is the only one on which either society or my life will work.

When we speak of God's will we too often think of nothing more than His wish that we should be good and conduct our life on honest and unselfish principles. It does not occur to us that all the detail of our life—what post we take, how we spend this £1, the use we make of this hour, whom we make friends with, every decision taken on wages or trade policy —are all significant for God, and will, in a really God-controlled life, be consciously related to His purpose for us and the world. Yet the God we see in the Bible is emphatically not the kind of parent who says to His children at the beginning of a day: 'Now you can go where you want and do what you like so long as you don't get your feet wet and do come back in time for dinner.' God has a more positive programme for us and a more intimate concern in our lives than that.

It is not only important for Him that Abraham should be a good man, but vital that he should leave his family home in Ur of the Chaldees and go to live in another country. A whole section of God's plan depends on whether Ananias is prepared to set aside

his fear, and pay that call in Straight Street, Damascus. It matters just as much to-day where John Smith, who has handed over his business to God, builds his new factory, or where Mr. and Mrs. Jones decide to live, now that they are letting God use their home. For God is an architect, planning a building—a building of reconstructed lives and a reconstructed society; and the place of every brick is of importance. God is a General directing a campaign—a campaign against evil; and the movement of each soldier is vital to His strategy. He does not want children who will just behave themselves and give Him no trouble. He wants willing co-operators who will allow Him to direct their lives in every detail, and to fit them together as a living part of His plan of reconstruction. It is when we are prepared to seek the will of God at this level that we shall find the answer to all our own problems, and the world's problems as well.

We are in great need of this discovery to-day.

We have tried our hand at the architecture of world-peace, and have failed. We are in the grip of economic forces which we can no longer control. The social structures we have built are crumbling. It is the hour of disillusion and helplessness and growing fear.

Behind all this lies the breakdown in countless individual lives. There are growing numbers of men and women who cannot adjust themselves to the strains and demands of life to-day. They are the victims of anxiety. They fail to solve the problems of sex, marriage and home life. They are oppressed by

the sense of futility in a life for which they have seen no purpose. They cannot understand themselves and are ill-adjusted to their surroundings and their work. Their real trouble is that they have been trying to run their lives in their own way, by their own wisdom, and in their own strength.

To such a generation, and to such men and women, frightened by the growing demonstration of their impotence, the message that God has a plan —detailed, comprehensive, adequate for every situation and every individual—is like a great shout of hope! With this discovery God comes right back into our lives as an active God who has an intimate concern in the smallest detail of our programme. It is He who is at work directing affairs; we are taking His orders.

But how can we actually receive this direction from God?

We must look for the answer to another of the great affirmations of our faith: *God speaks.* That is the tremendous fact around which both the Old and New Testaments are built—not that man can and may speak to God, but that God can and does speak to man.

Most of us, of course, believe that God speaks to us in a general way through Nature, through conscience, through reason, through circumstances, or through other people. But the Bible shows us a God who also speaks in a much more intimate, personal, and definite way to those who will listen and obey. The Old Testament is the story of men and women who believed that God told them what

to do and what to say in national affairs and personal dealings. In the New Testament a full relationship to God is described by saying that 'we receive the Holy Spirit.' If that phrase is vague to us, it was not vague to the writers of the New Testament. To those first Christians that gift clearly meant, not only the purifying and strengthening power of God within them, but His directing voice as well. He is the One who dictates their decisions in council. As their Master promised, they are given the words to say when called on to witness. Peter on the roof-top is told to go down and follow the messengers of Cornelius; Philip to 'get up and go south along the road from Jerusalem to Gaza'; and Paul is directed not to enter Bithynia. Here is a picture of men and women moving obediently under the effective guidance of God.

Is God less able to guide us to-day?

Actually there are thousands of men and women now who are making the experiment of seeking the same guidance in all the affairs of life, and are finding that, right out beyond their own powers of judgement and reasoning, God is able to give them an inward certainty as to what He wants them to do. And the results are incomparably better than when they ran their own lives in their own way.

This is what the head of a big manufacturing firm says about the results: 'My first revolutionary guidance was that I had to make a new price list. God showed me that it was wrong to use varying discounts and secret agreements. He also gave me the power to obey, because, as far as I could see it would cost

me my business. All the customers who at lunch had got a secret agreement, would go away. This new price list was made June 1, 1935, with the following results:

'(a) Increase in sales by £3,000; (b) Increase in profit by twenty per cent; (c) More orders than before by letter, as customers knew what the best prices were and did not wait for our salesman to quote special prices; (d) No fear of being away from my business, because the youngest girls can now give anyone the prices and conditions.

'I learned that: It is not a burden, but a privilege to have God with me in my business, because God knows more of real business than I.'

The results in other spheres of life are equally remarkable. An author recently told me that, following his decision to give his life to God, he found that he was doing twice the work in half the time. Now his 'reader' says that he must re-write five chapters written before his surrender, in order to bring them up to the level of those written since.

This is another of the truths we are needing to lay hold on afresh. The last generation relied on the adequacy of human reason. Even religious people talked as though reason was itself the voice of God. For the present generation that claim has been disproved by growing chaos. The Bible knows nothing of the adequacy of man's unaided reason. Our judgement is distorted. Our reasoning is very often only an elaborate means of justifying what we want to do; our decisions are dictated by fear, prejudice, feeling, and our disguised lusts. And none

of us can see the issues involved in our simplest act.

If we are to fit into God's plan for us, we have again and again to take steps for which it is impossible at the time to see the real reasons. We can only hope to live a life fully effective, and possessing a real sense of security and peace, if this truth that 'God speaks' can be tested and found true by us.

What if we can prove by experiment that God has a plan for European relations, for the coal-mining industry, for unemployment, and that statesmen, industrialists, social workers can get in touch with Him and learn it? What if He has a plan for my home, for my children's education, for my business, for my future? Then, not only is there the chance that I and a lot of people like me will find the solution of our difficulties and troubles, but there is a chance that God, through lives more fully under His control, will be able to build up the kind of world-order He wants.

God has a plan. God speaks.

But if He is to be heard and His plan is to be known and carried out, *man must listen.*

That means a new approach to God for many of us. Our attitude when we have prayed has been, 'Listen, Lord, for Thy servant speaketh.' Our prayer has been what Canon Streeter classifies as 'pagan' prayer—the attempt to bend God to our desires and make Him the servant of our needs. We have made our plans and decisions first, and then sought God's

blessing and assistance. Prayer, when it consists of this one-sided address by us to God, becomes increasingly unreal and is eventually dropped or only formally retained. Christian prayer begins with the desire to know God's will for us and be brought under His control. The promise that our petitions will be answered is only to those who have first placed themselves in line with His will. If God is to become for us the living, active God, at work directing our life and the world's, it is vital that we should learn how to listen.

There is one condition to be fulfilled before we begin. We must be willing to hear anything God says to us. It is useless to seek His guidance in one area of life when we are not prepared for Him to talk to us about a certain other area with which He needs to deal first. If we want guidance about our family, we may have to listen to some things God has to tell us about ourselves, our character and habits. If it is personal problems, worries, or health for which we need direction, we may have to face what God has to say about the way we run our business, or about our attitude to money. It is all or nothing. Before you begin to listen to God, you must get rid of any known reservations.

I remember a man who complained to me that he did not get any guidance when he tried having a 'quiet time.' A few questions brought out the fact that, actually, the name of his sister kept coming into his mind, but he had not given it any attention. A few more questions showed plainly why the name kept recurring. God was telling him to remake a

50

long-broken relationship. He had wanted other guidance. It is often so, but guidance must come along God's lines, not ours.

What next?

Our aim, remember, is to put our lives under God's control, and find out whether He can speak clearly enough in our hearts for us to know the steps He wants us to take. In all probability there are things in our lives which will have to be cleared up before God can really take control; and the first word God says to us will be about these. At any rate let us begin by sitting quietly for a few minutes thinking of our life in the light of what we already know of God's will.

The summary of Christ's teaching under the headings of Absolute Honesty, Absolute Purity, Absolute Unselfishness, Absolute Love, will help us. We shall not have been quiet very long before we know that God is putting His finger here, and here, where there has got to be a change, or where we must go and put matters straight with someone else. Perhaps a few minutes more quiet will make us sure at any rate of the first practical step to take. Our first experiment is made.

If we want to go on with it we had better carry out these first orders which have come to us, for God can only continue to speak to us if we obey. Disobedience blocks the line.

Probably our first 'quiet times' will bring us mostly these personal convictions and steps. The way between us and God needs clearing. It also needs keeping clear, and every day we shall first listen for God's correction.

But we are trying to discover whether God can *direct* as well as *correct* us. Let us now make the experiment of bringing under review some of our practical concerns.

We have certain decisions to make to-day in our business or our home. Let us quietly turn over in our minds all the factors we know which should influence our decision, setting on one side the thoughts that are prompted by fear or pride or self-interest, letting the thought of what God would want penetrate deeper into our judgement, waiting for the growing conviction as to the right step to take. If we are prepared to do this patiently and thoroughly and to bring under review all areas of our life—our business, home, leisure, money, time, relationships, health—we shall be surprised at what comes to us, the new certainty in our decisions, the new sense of direction, and the growing assurance that God is in control. A very busy housewife with a husband, three children, and a martyr-complex previously found life complicated and wearying. She now says, 'I found when I began to spend an hour daily in quiet, that far from taking up precious time and adding to an already heavy programme, that hour became the simplifying, unifying, time-saving key to the whole day.'

These are two practical ways in which we can experiment. The important thing is for us to make, each for himself, the thrilling discovery that God has spoken to us. Once we have made that discovery, God will shape our 'quiet times' and develop them until they express a full personal relationship with

Him, and include our thanksgiving, worship, petition, intercession, as part of our life with Him. We are only talking now of how to begin.

What can we expect as we grow more experienced in this listening to God? Probably the first thing we realize will be that the whole level of our thinking has been altered. We shall see that what we took for sound reasoning before was just our human thinking, dictated by self-will, prejudice, fear, or limited by the fact that we were leaving God out of the reckoning. The judgement of a surrendered man who listens to God is something more than human reason. It may often seem, as Paul says, sheer folly to other people.

This does not mean that, when we have a 'quiet time,' we resign our reasoning powers. The idea that listening to God means making your mind a blank is a curious misconception which has hindered many people. It does mean that you leave room for God to lead you beyond your human thoughts, and tell you things you could never know yourself.

The next thing we shall find is that we are able better to interpret God's other ways of speaking to us through circumstances, through other people, through the Bible. We are learning to know His voice in our 'quiet time,' and we recognize it better elsewhere.

We shall probably find also that from time to time there come to us clear suggestions about something we should do, or somewhere we should go. Often they have a strong, impelling force about them, and

if we neglect them they come back insistently. I remember one day, returning by car from a friend's wedding, I found that I had two hours to spare. There is no doubt about the way in which they would have been spent before I discovered that God has a plan for every minute. The open moors were near by, and it was June. A 'quiet time' by the roadside, however, brought the clear guidance to call on the editor of a daily newspaper, whose house was a few miles away. The result, two months later, was a leading article which made a real contribution to preparing public opinion for a Christian solution to national problems. That God does guide us in this direct way has been proved far too often to be doubted.

Of course, every thought that comes to us in the 'quiet time' is not God's guidance. We need to test the voices that come to us along a line that has been so long disused or blocked. We have immediate cause to reject promptings which conflict with what we already know of His will. Nothing which is unloving, impure, dishonest, or selfish comes from God. Other suggestions which come to us may have to be talked out with some experienced person who knows how to listen to God. In other cases we may have to wait for clearer conviction in our own minds. Sometimes the only test is to make the venture and act. We shall make mistakes. But an honest mistake is of far more use to God than the timid inaction which makes no venture. God never fails to use an honest mistake, so that we and others learn from it more of His will and how to interpret that will better.

The guided life is a growth. Through the continuous experiment of listening to God, more and more of our thinking and action is freed from the guidance of self, hate, fear, indulgence, prejudice, ignorance, and all other forms of sin, and is made available to God.

And *this guidance does work.* That is its final confirmation.

Listening to God takes time. It takes a lot more time than the brief address to God which we call 'saying our prayers.'

It takes time because God has to get down through so many layers of our human, self-governed, sin-dulled thinking before He can communicate His thoughts to us. It takes time because God leads us in 'quiet time' into the thorough constructive planning of our life in partnership with Him. It is true that God intends us to live in such contact with Him that He can speak to us at any time; but the men and women who have known Him best have invariably found that they could not maintain that constant touch without daily time spent alone and quiet with Him. No one can live a full and vital Christian life who does not set aside a daily period for this quiet fellowship with God. Most of us, when we say we have not time, are simply dishonest. Some of us have not realized how much time later in the day is saved through added efficiency, through clearer selection of what is important and what should be left, through the greater strength and peace which come when we have listened to God and received His directions for our day.

And morning is emphatically the best time. The

opening of the day with quiet thought, planning, and prayer, is so obviously the right start for the Christian that it hardly needs the backing of the universal experience of the men and women who have lived nearest God in every century.

Nearly all the objections from men and women in normal health resolve themselves into an objection to getting up earlier. Their difficulty is either laziness, undisciplined lateness the night before, or a sluggish physical condition which will disappear in a few weeks of new discipline and more careful attention to health. But we are on a quest which must not be held up by such things as these. We are seeking God-controlled lives and a God-controlled world. No second-best in the time we give to listening to God will suffice.

How long ought we to spend? That is a question which will decide itself for every honest adventurer in God-controlled living. As God carries a man out into fuller action and responsibility the question is turned round. It is now, 'How much time can I get?' not 'How little will do?'

One practical hint is well worth taking. Use a note-book and pencil. Put down the thoughts which come in 'quiet time.' A typist who appeared minus her note-book when her employer wanted to dictate letters, would not hold her post long. It would not help her to plead that she could remember everything without taking it down. There is no reason why we should be less efficient with God. The Chinese say that the strongest memory is weaker than the palest ink.

We are being called to prove effectively for our world to-day that God has a plan—for the world, for His Church, for me; that He can communicate it in definite, detailed, adequate guidance to those who are willing to obey; and that His plan is the complete answer to chaos, whether public or private.

The price is our willingness to listen.

III

BREAKING BARRIERS AND
BUILDING BRIDGES

Barriers!

In that one word more than half the trouble of the world is expressed.

We are living in a divided world. Every day brings news of the war of nations, of classes, or of economic groups. Self-interest, fear, bitter memory, national pride are splitting the human family into isolated fragments. Co-operation, which is the world's most urgent need, becomes increasingly difficult.

Such a world of isolated groups, eyeing each other with growing suspicion over rising walls of mis-understanding, can only be the product of individuals who do not know how to live together. Selfishness, fear, resentment, pride, do not live in the air. They live in men. They only move States because they have the power to move us. We must look for the barriers which separate nations and classes, first in ourselves and our homes, and then in our daily contacts with those around us.

When we do look for those barriers close at hand their existence is evident enough. One man has described his home as 'a filling-station by day and a parking place at night.' That might stand as the classic description of thousands of homes to-day. They are places where a number of people live under the same roof and feed at the same table, but hardly know anything of what is going on under the surface of each other's lives. Husband and wife have been

divided by all the accumulated reticences of years. The children are walled off from their parents by resentment of parental domination and lack of understanding. The parents themselves are shut in by their self-pity and exasperation at what seems the self-will and thoughtlessness of their children. Brothers and sisters, shy of one another, go each their own way.

Outside the home the same story is carried on. At school the child is too often afraid to tell his real difficulties to the teacher. He is afraid of being laughed at or punished. In the office men and women work together without getting to know each other. Jealousy, fear, incompatibility split them into cliques or leave one and another standing alone. In the factory the 'boss' is a remote and unknown being who only descends into the lives of the work-people when something is wrong.

These are the raw materials of a divided world.

People who do not know each other and have little inkling of each other's difficulties or aims, cannot create a united world. They are certain to misinterpret each other. Sooner or later they will quarrel.

The most frequent reason for our isolation is fear. It is fear which makes us hide.

We are afraid of many things. We fear the loss of reputation. We think that if other people saw what we are really like, they would laugh at our mistakes and despise us for our failures. So we cover up our mistakes and failures with silence or self-excuse. We pose as confident, when we are

nothing of the kind. The face we present to the world is really a mask.

We are afraid in business. We are expecting the other man to steal a march on us. So we work in the dark. We are not going to give him the chance to get in first. We disguise our intentions. And thus we help to create the atmosphere of suspicion and mistrust in which the world lives.

We are afraid of being found out and compelled to let go some of our practices or some of our relationships. If our family only knew—if our business associates or employers only knew—there would have to be a change. We do not want to change. We should hate to change. And so those little reticences and petty deceptions begin and grow until we are living two lives—the one other people see and the one we hope they do not see!

Frankness, trust, understanding, free and happy co-operation cannot exist between people who are hiding from each other.

We greatly need to come out into the open— to take off the mask and drop the pose, and to be our real selves, honest about our mistakes and sins, frank about our thoughts and intentions, willing to let other people know us. Isolated, secretive living is bad for the world and bad for us. It not only builds barriers between us and those we live with, but it shuts us in on ourselves and breeds the loneliness, morbidity, repression and distorted outlook from which a great deal of our mental and spiritual sickness comes.

When a man does come out into the open in all

his relationships with others, the effect is revolutionary. A journalist apologizes to the assembled pressmen of another country for the bitterness of his articles, and at once a door is opened to new understanding between two nations. A statesman admits in an international council that his country's policy has been mistaken and offers reconsideration of the issue, and immediately a breath of fresh air blows through world affairs. The representative of a large firm puts all his cards on the table before his competitors, and a threatened price war is called off. A father who has tried many ways of getting his daughter to be frank comes off his pedestal and begins telling her of some of his own difficulties. The prompt and unhesitating response is a flood of confidences and the beginning of a new relationship. Two brothers have long been careful only to let each other see selected portions of their lives. They discover that in this life-long game of hide-and-seek, they have actually been fighting a lonely battle against the same temptations; now they tell each other of their victories and defeats.

These are real people, from a growing company of men and women who are breaking down barriers and creating new relationships by their simple honesty about themselves. They are prepared to pocket their pride, risk their reputation, hazard their material interests, for the sake of living in the open with their fellows. They are creating a new atmosphere in every community into which they go. They are breaking down the barriers, and opening up the way—the way to a different world.

In this different world we shall not only *know* each other; we shall *trust* each other.

You cannot work with other men satisfactorily unless you trust them and they trust you. You will not trust them while you suspect that they have an axe of their own to grind. They will not trust you while you are holding on to anything which you are not willing to yield up for the common good. It is this holding on to our own private aims, our own private interests, our own private possessions which splits up any community. It divides nation or family into separate and competing factions and individuals, who only hold together so long as their interests do not clash.

A belief in the other man's disinterestedness is the only basis on which men and women can live and work together in an unbreakable fellowship. The real problem of life to-day is to create trust.

Imagine for a moment an international conference, a meeting of employers and employees, a Church committee, or just two people seeking the settlement of a dispute, where each believes the other to be entirely free from private aims, and concerned with nothing but the common interest of both sides! What need to say more? At that level the major problems of mankind disappear.

Trust is not created by waiting for the other man. It begins to form and grow around those who give themselves utterly to other people. Jesus' answer to a divided world was to give the whole of Himself to others, and so to create around Him a little community where trust and co-operation had been

generated by self-giving. That community—at first only twelve men—was the growing point of the new world. The living cells of the new world to-day will be companies of men and women, in home, business, town, and nation, who have learned to trust each other and live without barriers.

There is no other solution. There is no other way by which the creative love of God can get out into the world to form a new trusting relationship between men, except through a self-giving like Christ's.

It must be like Christ's; substitutes do not work. Many of us give to other people, but we give 'things' and not 'ourselves.' There are plenty of employers who give their workpeople good wages and a bright welfare-centre, but no personal interest and concern such as would establish a real relationship of confidence. There are parents who give their children a comfortable home and a good education, but keep themselves spiritually remote. There are lots of us who give the money to meet all kinds of needs in other people, but fail to meet their deepest need of friendship. And when we do try to help others in their personal problems we give them good advice from a slightly elevated pedestal, instead of laying beside them our own deepest experiences of God and sin, of victory and defeat, so that first they lose their loneliness and then they begin to see, through our confidences, how God deals with a need like theirs.

Self-giving will certainly mean that our time and money, and our strength, are entirely at the disposal of other people as God directs, so that those others begin to realize that we shall withhold nothing from

them for selfish reasons, or because we shirk the cost. One of the characteristics of Jesus was this complete availability. But real self-giving will mean that we make available to men more than our time and strength and possessions. It will mean that we are prepared to share with them the innermost core of our life—our temptations, our difficulties, our sins, and discoveries of God—if these can be used to help them and bring them to God.

Our self-giving is not complete until no pride or fear, no pain or shame, will prevent us giving all of ourselves to another in his need.

People sometimes say, 'Oh, but these things are too sacred to talk about!' In all too many cases that is the defence of people who have precious little to tell, and whose experience of God is not vivid and joyful enough to make them want to pass it on. In other cases it is a form of spiritual selfishness. How should we have had the story of the Temptation in the Wilderness, the glimpse into the disquieted soul of Jesus as He saw the approaching end, or the most intimate words of Gethsemane, unless Jesus had told His secrets to the disciples? How could we have learned what God could do with a man like Paul unless Paul himself had been willing to tell, humbly and honestly, what he was like before God changed him? We are under an unpayable debt to men like St. Augustine, Brother Lawrence, John Wesley, and a great unnamed company of men and women who have been willing to let us see, in the inner history of their own souls, how God deals with sin.

It is self-giving at this level which establishes the deepest and strongest personal relationships between men and women, and it was on the basis of such relationships that Christ proposed to build the new world. The fellowship thus created was to be in the world what Paul described as 'a colony of heaven,' a centre of civilizing power. This is the function of the real Church. We are rather apt to confuse the Church with the loose associations of men and women who happen to worship in the same building, or meet each other in the running of various organizations, but many of whom hardly know each other's names and have little interchange beyond remarks about the weather. These associations are not 'Churches.' They are 'potential Churches,' and often have a nucleus of men and women in real fellowship with each other. But the living, functioning Church of Christ exists only where men and women are really giving themselves to each other in unreserved personal relationships.

It is this kind of fellowship that the Christian is called to create around him. Nothing less will save the world from chaos.

This way of living, which breaks down barriers and builds up trust, can be conveniently described in one word—*Sharing*.

Sharing can be defined as being honest with other people about yourself. It means being willing (for God's purposes) to give the whole of yourself to anyone. It does not mean telling everything about yourself to everybody you meet. It does mean being willing to tell anything to anyone—if God

shows you that your sharing can be useful in establishing a new and deeper relationship, or in helping another person to find God.

Real sharing can be very costly. If some of us are to restore the right relationship with those round us —perhaps a husband, a wife, a child; perhaps those who work with or for us; perhaps someone who attends the same Church—it will mean facing crucifixion. To let them see what we are really like will cost no less. And if we are going to let God take us right into the lives of other people, with the love that pours itself out to them, it will mean the Cross again. To share *Himself* with the world meant that for Christ. The price of redeeming relationships with men and women is always the Cross.

Sharing has to be learnt. We cannot really make ourselves known to others until we have been introduced to ourselves, and one of the serious effects of our reserve and spiritual isolation is that we have become strangers to our own souls. God has to bring us right out into the light, where we can see ourselves stripped of self-deception and face the naked truth about our actions, our thoughts and our motives.

One of God's most effective ways of introducing us to ourselves is to send us to another person, whom we can trust, to tell them the whole truth about our lives as far as we know it. Quite apart from the fact that it is a healthy and liberating thing to unburden ourselves, the necessity of putting into words to another person the hard facts about our sin makes us see it more clearly and hate it more thoroughly. Besides which, the other person will probably see

things in us to which we are blind, and will help us to see them. God has given us this invaluable gift of fellowship as one of the most effective means to real self-knowledge, penitence, and new life and we lose something vital if we shrink from the humiliating but liberating experience.

If we are to go on being honest with others we must go on being honest with ourselves. Life moves ahead and fresh discoveries about ourselves have to be made, fresh difficulties faced, or sins confessed. That is why we must seek frequent fellowship of the kind in which we can talk over these discoveries without reserve. If we cannot find this quality of fellowship with several people, we can begin with one, so long as we do not remain content with one.

Sharing of this kind is thoroughly wholesome if it is seen as a means of keeping spiritually fit and free for God's use, and if it issues in practical steps to put right what is wrong. It keeps the system free from any accumulation of poisons.

It is as we learn in this way to be honest with ourselves and others, to take off the mask and drop the pose, to step out from behind our reserve and pride, that we become citizens of God's new world —men and women around whom a new honesty and trust begins to grow.

When we learn to share, each of us becomes a living cell in that new world.

IV

LIFE-CHANGING

CHRIST called men, not just to a life in which He met their need, but to one in which they joined Him in His task. In vivid and homely language which would stir the imagination of fishermen, He asks Simon and Andrew to join Him in an amazing fishing expedition. The catch was to be men.

It is very important that we should get this clear. The Christian life involves necessarily the fullest identification of ourselves with Christ in His supreme work of bringing men and women to God. To be a Christian is to be a friend of Christ; and to speak of being the friend of anyone when we do not care for the thing he cares for, or join him in the thing he is living for, is simply meaningless.

Christ lived and died to change men, by bringing them to a definite personal trust in and obedience to God. He knew that nothing less would meet their real needs, and nothing less would be sufficient to redeem and remake the world. To stop short of that would be to fail. Unless, then, we are prepared to let Him draw us into a share in the same passion and the same programme, we are no real friends of His, since there can be no unity of mind and heart between us.

Deep in our minds to-day is the idea that the Christian life is primarily a matter of being good oneself, and being ready to help others in what we call practical ways. To deal with their deepest needs and win them for God is the parson's job—or at any

rate the job of people with special gifts. That is to mistake the real nature of Christian life and service. No doubt Christ meets us first at the level of our own need. He stoops to us in the tangle of our problems—reaches to us while we are still centred in ourselves; but He cannot give us His full answer, even for our own needs, until we let Him lift us, self-forgotten, into partnership with Him in His redemptive love of men. Release from ourselves and with it new power, can only come fully in that active companionship.

Not only our own life but our service of men will be stunted if we stop short of this work of life-changing with Christ. We may meet people's material needs, we may aid them in sickness or misfortune, we may provide healthy interests and sound instruction for them—and yet fall short of the full Christian answer to their need. Christian 'philanthropy' is not enough. If we love men at all, we shall be prepared to do these lesser things for them when it seems right and wise. If we love men as Christ loved them, we shall not be content until they have been so brought into touch with God that they are themselves remade, and have, in their own lives, the full answer to their needs. The world to-day provides ample evidence of the inadequacy of humanitarian service which stops short of changing the man himself.

For we must remember that the love of Christ, which we are called to share, is an active love. He was not content to live a life of 'silent witness' and hope for the best. He went out seeking men. When we are filled with the same kind of love we shall do

as He did. Life-changing is not a matter of special commission nor of special gifts. It is a matter of how much real love for people we have, how much we want them to find the one complete answer to their need, and how much of God we have ourselves to share with them.

When we have this real love for people, the office and the factory, the home and the school, and every place where the daily business of life is carried on, will become the scene of life-changing. An hotel proprietor in the South of England meets every day with several of his staff to plan, under the guidance of God, how his hotel may become a place where the guests find not only comfort and rest, but God. A Dutch lawyer, who handled divorce cases in the courts, now settles many of them in his office by showing his clients how God can reconstruct their lives. Many doctors now know how to cure their patients more thoroughly, because they have learned the secret of healing the mind as well as the body.

Life-changing is simply normal Christian living. It is doing Christ's work. If our aim falls below that level we are failing Him.

It is very tempting for us, confronted by this high call, to find excuses for our failure, and to reassure ourselves in the fact that at least we are serving others in good ways, if not the highest.

Before we allow ourselves to venture up these side-tracks of excuse we should do well to ask ourselves some honest questions.

Have I ever seriously faced this responsibility?

Am I actually willing for God to take me right
   into the centre of other people's lives, or do
   I shrink from the cost of being involved?
Do I care enough whether they find God or not?
Have I enough conviction that the one thing
   people need most is a personal relationship
   with God?
Am I held back by the knowledge of things in my
   own life which have not been uncompromis-
   ingly faced?
Do I fear the opinion of others or the loss of their
   friendship?

And let us beware of pleading our unfitness for so
wonderful and sacred a task as dealing with the inner
life of men. That is not humility. It is distrust of
the One who has called us, and with whom all things
are possible—even the miracle of my being used to
bring another person to God. Until these issues have
been faced it is too soon to conclude that life-changing is not our calling.

We cannot change another person. Apart from
the fact that God is already at work in the other
person's life, making him aware of need, awakening
responses, and in the end convincing him of the truth
of what he has heard and the rightness of the new
steps he sees, any effort of ours will be quite useless.
Anyone who has tried it knows that human argu-
ment and persuasion do not change people's hearts.
But, in the ceaseless work God is carrying on in the

100

lives of men, He does fit us in when we fulfil the conditions.

The first condition is our own simple honesty. If we try to hand on to other people something we have not got ourselves, it will be no wonder if they are unimpressed. People are drawn and captured by something they can see has really happened to us. It is not that we are consciously dishonest; but we present to others the belief and the experience we feel we ought to have, rather than those we actually have. Pride creeps in, and we pass quickly over the gaps in our knowledge of God. Or perhaps we are afraid that, if the other person sees the meagreness of our Christian life, he will not be attracted; and consequently we pitch the note of our witness higher than is justified by fact, or resort to giving good advice instead of honestly telling the other person the things which are real to us. In either case the note rings false.

God does not reach other people so much through our opinions, and our advice as through the rock-bottom facts of our life, honestly presented. It is reality which is redemptive.

I have known a man, only an hour old in the Christian life, bring another man to God simply because he was honest about the facts of his own surrender. The first price of life-changing is this kind of honesty.

The second condition is that we should be really interested in people. When our interest ceases to be centred in ourselves or the small circle of our particular friends, and we begin to take a real interest

in the varied folk we meet, we see a whole new range of opportunities for entering other people's lives, and every encounter becomes a responsibility given us by God.

God cannot use many of us deeply in the lives of other people because we do not see. And we do not see because we are not interested. Christ was intensely interested in people. In other words, He loved them. We shall not share in His redemptive work with men and women unless we too love them. Life-changing can never be performed as a duty. It is something which happens when we are deeply and sincerely interested in people.

The other condition of God's using us in changing lives is that we should be guided. As we saw, a changed life is the result of what God has been doing in a man's mind and heart. We are only of use if we fit in at the time and in the way which dovetails into what God is already doing for the man. If we try to gate-crash a man's soul before the door is ajar, or try to hurry him ahead of the convictions God is bringing home to him, we merely spoil God's work. We need to know when to speak and when to be silent, what to say and what to leave unsaid, when to step aside and give the other man time to think, and when to press him relentlessly towards decision. These things pass the wit of the wisest of us. They are only made clear to us through a sensitiveness to people and their needs which is born in prayer. God cannot guide us rightly in individual work unless we pray for people and listen for His directions about them.

104

We must be guided too in the choice of those in whose lives God wishes to use us. God cares for everyone, and His ultimate purpose is to bring all who are willing, into a full life, but, in carrying out that purpose, He does choose the men and women whom He needs next as leaders. It may, therefore, be much more important for me to spend hours with some man or woman on whom the lot of hundreds of others depends, than to run about after a dozen people who are not God's next work for me. God has His strategy, and it may be vital for a whole community that the 'salient' of a single life should be captured before any wide advance is possible. It may be a business man (or a workman), who, when changed, will be able to carry out God's plan in a whole industry, a teacher who will open the way to a God-controlled school, a local 'tough' who will win all his 'tough' friends, a politician who will set a new level of national policy. And God can tell me, if I listen, who is my responsibility.

These are not conditions which can only be fulfilled by the few and the specially gifted. They are the simple and spiritual conditions which can be fulfilled by anyone who is willing to learn in the school of Christ.

The vital element in this work of life-changing is, of course, an infectious experience of God—an experience real enough for other people to catch from us. The conditions we have to fulfil are the simple and spiritual conditions just outlined. If,

however, we are to be used by God to the fullest extent in other people's lives, there is much to be learned in the art of dealing with men and women. Our own practical experience is the best teacher, but it may be some help if we summarize a few lessons learned by those who have attempted the work themselves.

One thing must be grasped at the beginning. If we are to help men and women deeply, we must make friends with them. People only begin to show themselves to us when they feel they can trust us. They only trust us if they feel we care for them, and understand them as real persons, and are not merely interested in them as 'cases' or as 'possible converts.' To establish such a personal relationship needs patience and makes big demands. We shall have to find time, put ourselves out of our way to cultivate acquaintance, get to know what other persons are interested in, what books they read, what are their ambitions. We may have to join them in their play. Sometimes the entry on the other life is swift and the response to us instinctive. Sometimes the process is long. But whether the process is long or short, if we try to break in without friendship, attempt to put the other persons right and tell them what they should believe or do, we shall find the door of their inner life slammed in our face. If we are to work at this deep level, then we must reckon with the fact of sex. There are confidences which can only rightly be shared between man and man, and woman and woman. To ignore this condition would mean either a superficial job, or a wrong relationship.

108

It is when we have made friends that we begin to see the other man more clearly. That is essential. The first step in life-changing is to introduce a man to himself. We have to help him to look behind his actions and his feelings and see their roots, or perhaps face things in his life he has been hiding so long that now he cannot see them. That is a task which requires the insight of real love. The difficulty he brings to us first may be (and very often is) a mere blind. Again and again people will put forward their intellectual difficulties when their real trouble is moral; or they will tell you a lot of things of which they are afraid, while keeping back the deepest fear of their lives. Sin deceives a man about himself, and our first work is to help in breaking through that self-deception. It is here that we can so easily fail those we are trying to help. We can fail through carelessness because we simply have not taken the trouble to watch and learn the other man as far as we possibly can.

We can fail through sentimentality. Either our human affection for the other person, or our dislike of going too deep into our own life, leads us to idealize, to soften down harsh facts, or to stay the probe. We call it being charitable. Actually it is sheer betrayal, and the other person may have cause one day to curse us for our lack of the kind of love which loves enough to hurt. We can fail through haste. We seize on the symptoms of the trouble and haven't the patience to get down to causes. A good deal depends on the thoroughness with which we have faced ourselves. It is not only that honest self-

knowledge helps us in the diagnosis of others, but our own deepest discoveries about ourselves, shared with him, may be what is needed to help the other man to see himself.

The outcome of this work of helping a man to become acquainted with himself should be his own willing confession of all he has so far seen.

The next stage will test our restraint. Our human impulse is to give advice, to point out the steps that other persons ought to take, to rearrange their life ourselves. Actually the only thing we can rightly do is to help them to listen, not to us, but to God. Somewhere at the base of their life God is speaking to them, convicting them about the past and insistently pointing the new way. It is tremendously important that they should discover this themselves. If they listen to us instead of to God, they will depend on us instead of Him. That is fatal. We must do no more at this stage than help them to listen for the deepest voices in their own souls, until they know that God is speaking and make their first response in trust and obedience to Him alone.

When the other person has arrived at this point and is face to face with steps to be taken, and a call to be answered, we must be ready lovingly and firmly to hold them up to the decision that must be made. Most people try to run away when they reach this stage. They try to postpone the decision, though they know it must be made. They try to make it by instalments, or offer to face any other steps except the one which really matters. A friend who will not let them run away is invaluable. It is wise also to remember

how much it helps if the decision is put into words—
perhaps the words of a prayer as we kneel with our
friend. We should see, too, that the one who has
surrendered makes the fact known as soon as possible
to other people. Anything vague and indefinite
about the act of surrender is a source of later
weakness.

There follows a very demanding part of our work
for men and women. Surrender to God has begun
the new life, but the one we have helped so far, needs
the most patient aid in working out the implications
of that surrender, establishing a new discipline of
life, making necessary restitutions for the past, and
getting into action for God.

It is a crime to expose new-born babies. It is an
even worse crime to leave our spiritual children
without careful individual attention. We are too
easily content to push them into a job in the Church
or urge them to attend meetings—mistaking attend-
ance at meetings for real Christian fellowship.
Fellowship is always between two individuals. It
can only exist in a company of people when it
already exists between the individuals composing the
company. We shall, then, need to keep in close
touch with these spiritual children of ours, helping
them to see the fuller implications of their surrender,
and particularly planning with them daring action;
for fellowship is found most of all when we step into
God-guided action together. An employer and one
of his workmen plan how to put the whole factory
under the guidance of God. Men, who were
previously trade rivals, seek God's plan for the

industry in which they are engaged. A number of people, seeing their responsibility for their city, plan its capture for God. In such action fellowship becomes real, and our spiritual muscles are stretched in healthy growth.

This, then, is the quality of redemptive living to which Christ calls all who are willing to share in His work for men. It is a partnership which will drain us to the bottom, taking far more than we have. But it is in this work, which is utterly impossible to us, that we make the greatest discoveries of the sufficiency of God.

This work of life-changing is in the end the only contribution which we Christians have to make towards a new world. Anything less than loving men and women into personal relationship with God will fail.

V

CHRISTIAN REVOLUTION

THE most striking characteristic of the ordinary man to-day is his helplessness.

He is the bewildered spectator of events over which he has apparently no control, but which affect him profoundly. A troubled rumour spreads through the markets of the world, and he finds the value of his savings halved or his employment gone. He watches the drift of political policy that he knows may land him and his family into the unspeakable horrors of another war, and he sees nothing that he can do about it. When he does try to do something and goes to the poll to vote into office a new government, he reaps results that bear little relation to the promises of the election platform. He joins a Peace organization, but when the echoes of the speeches he hears at its demonstrations die away, he can hear louder than ever the noise of the forge and factory where the nations are making the weapons of new warfare.

He does not, of course, live with his helplessness all the time. He could not bear it. He must escape, and does so in different ways. It may be into forgetfulness—the forgetfulness either of self-centred pleasure or of self-centred piety. A man can shut out the world and its urgency at a cinema or a dance. He can leave it out of count while he seeks his individual salvation.

On the other hand, he may escape from the sense of helplessness into some form of practical social

service. He may bestir himself to do something, without having any very clear sense of direction or any great confidence that what he is doing will prove effective. But it relieves him to be in action.

This is the simple truth about millions of ordinary men and women all over the world. Whether they are contriving to forget about it most of the time, or to reassure themselves by activity, the background of their life is the sense of frustration and impotence. If they are sustained by any hope, it is the vague hope—so near to despair—that something will happen somehow, or that someone else will do something about it. In any case, whatever is going to happen does not seem to have any real connexion with anything that they as individuals can do.

This is the paralysis that grips the world. It has also gripped the one body of men and women who should have the answer to paralysis—the Christian Church. So few people are left with any strong and impelling faith that their individual lives and actions have significance beyond themselves, and can avail in the bringing of a new and liberated world. The task of changing the world appears so gigantic and so remote that it daunts any attempt to make a personal contribution towards it. Unless we can demonstrate to men and women that there is a real way of remaking the world, and that they can become effective partners in it, they will remain the helpless spectators of the drift to destruction. The sheer weight of their inaction will quicken its pace.

What is the basis of the Christian hope of a new world? What part have I in its making?

The hope of a new world, which men and women of the pre-war generation entertained, was based either on a general faith in the inevitability of progress—a faith born in a partial understanding of the scientific doctrine of evolution; or on their confidence in the inventive genius and organizing capacity of man. Both foundations have given way.

The Christian hope of a new world has nothing in common with these exploded beliefs. The only way by which a new human society can come into being is by *the action of God*. As He created the world, so He can re-create it when men give Him the chance by their obedience.

When man obeys, God works.

We should lock up in an asylum a man who attempted to make a field of wheat by assembling thousands of stalks and leaves, planting them out laboriously, and sticking each grain on with gum. A waving field of corn is a miracle of life. It is the miracle which happens when man learns to do his part of simple obedience to the laws of growth, and ploughs the soil and scatters the seed. The difference is as great between man's attempt to reorganize society and God's recreation of it.

Two years ago the people of Norway were facing anxious social and moral problems, and attempting to deal with them along the lines of legislation. The attempt was not proving notably successful. Some time previously a woman over seventy years old, faced, in China, the call of God to go and live in Geneva. She obeyed. As a result the President of

the Norwegian Parliament, visiting Geneva, met
the challenge to put life under the guidance of
God. Later he invited thirty men and women to
visit Norway, and bring the same message of
God-guided living. In six months the principal
papers of the country and many leaders of its life
were bearing witness to a change in the mental
outlook of its people. A general strike which had
been pending did not take place. A remarkable
change in the atmosphere of Parliament was noticed
at the beginning of the next session. A celebrated
journalist apologized to Denmark for his bitter article
on the fisheries dispute, and opened the way to a new
understanding between the two nations. The President of the Authors' Club wrote a new kind of play,
which brought dramatic art into the service of
national regeneration. It drew very large audiences.

These are swift and partial glimpses at the rebirth of a nation. Politics, social life, morals, and
culture can be reborn when the creative power of
God is released by the obedience of one person.

Something happens. *When man obeys, God works.*

The new civilization which will replace our fast-
perishing social structure will be a miracle of God's
creative power working through men and women
surrendered to His will. That is the basis of our
hope—'a city whose builder and maker is God.'

This means that my relation as an individual to
the world-task becomes totally different. I am not
one utterly insignificant builder amongst countless
hosts, adding one brick to the gigantic structure of a
new world-order which, at that rate, will take incon-

128

ceivably long to complete. If such were the case, it would seem hardly worth while to bother with my brick in a world of such immediate urgency. Rather, my obedience to God can be like the closing of a switch which allows the current of His power to flow through a whole circuit of lives, blow up a mass of evil, weld together in new relationship two lives or a community, or set in motion far-reaching changes in men, in industry, in education, or any other area of human activity. My part as an ordinary man in the task of world reconstruction can thus be immediate and vital.

The effect of my unreserved obedience to the guidance of God cannot be calculated by any human arithmetic, either in its extent or its speed. A new factor has been introduced into the situation which completely alters it. God is in action.

What happens when men begin to seek and obey the guidance of God is not just an improvement in the present situation. God is not content to settle our strikes, resolve our family disputes, ease the tension of an international situation, restore equilibrium, and send us back to live more peaceably and comfortably a life on the old man-made lines. That is the extent of many people's ambition. It is not the extent of God's.

When men obey Him a revolution begins which will eventually change the whole structure of human society. When Philemon, obeying God, received back his runaway slave, Onesimus, as a brother, he did not merely re-establish his domestic equilibrium and resolve the difficulties caused for his wife by a

reduced staff: he started a social revolution. He did the thing which struck at the very foundations of the society in which he lived, based as it was on domestic slavery. And before many years were gone *the system* was changed, and an area of human life was reorganized.

The Christian hope of a new world only differs from the other revolutionary programmes which are being urged upon us to-day in two respects: It goes further; and its method is entirely different. The changes in human society which a living Christianity will bring about will make Communism and Fascism look pale and anæmic. An employer of labour a few years ago put his business wholly under God's direction. Recently a Labour leader wrote of him: 'He has done more, voluntarily, for his employees than any revolutionary Government would force him to do.'

The method of the Christian revolution is simple, unreserved obedience to God.

The head of an oil-refining firm, called to a conference on the testing of quality in oils, felt that in order to secure the most effective tests in the public interest he should reveal to his trade-rivals the carefully guarded secrets of manufacture by which he had built up his business. He did so: and at the same moment struck a blow at the foundations of the competitive system as we know it.

One of the representatives of Great Britain at the Washington Conference in 1922, after leaving the Conference temporarily to carry out official duties in Canada, felt guided to return to Washington and

look into the matter of a clause in the Pacific Treaty. He arrived just in time to give the necessary help in producing the final draft of a clause which has worked out satisfactorily ever since. He introduced into world politics a principle which will eventually destroy the old diplomacy, and replace international bargaining by God's control of world affairs.

Those who know the industrial North will realize how the protracted efforts to reorganize the cotton industry have been slowed again and again by the difficulty in getting all parties to suit their own interests and points of view. Earlier this year in Denmark, nine textile manufacturers sought together in quiet and prayer God's scheme of reorganization for their industry. They began a revolution in industrial affairs.

A departmental manager of a large industrial concern in the North of England began to listen to God. A dispute between himself and the employees in his department threatened to end in a strike. He considered the question in the new light of God's Plan, and listened to God's guidance. A possible solution came to his mind. He suggested it to the men, who welcomed it. 'We have never reached an agreement so quickly before, in fifteen years of negotiation,' said the men's representative, a prominent Trade Union leader. A revolution in the relationships of employer and employee had begun.

When men do such things anything can happen, because God comes in. And the only alternative to violent revolution which will shatter the structure of a society that fails to supply the human needs, or

respect the human rights of so many of its members, is a Divine re-creation of society which outdoes in thoroughness and outpaces in speed anything which violence can achieve. Such a revolution begins in the personal revolution of surrendering the whole of life and all its business to God's control.

Why, it may be asked, has Christianity so far failed in our generation to produce this revolution in society, and has consequently left the field open for revolution by violence?

Our obedience has not gone far enough, either in extent or cost.

Too often, men and women have come into an initial experience of God which has liberated them from their more obvious sins, but has left them tied still to their social environment and to their own unrecognized sins. They have taken part of their new life from their new Lord, but have continued to draw heavily on the conventional ideas and standards of their social or business world in the ordering of their conduct. They have renounced, it may be, sins of the flesh and the habits about which they were already uneasy in conscience, but have continued under the domination of their fears, their desire for security, their love of comfort, and their selfish independence of others. They did let God over their front doorstep, but kept Him standing in the vestibule.

Christian revolution begins when a man is really willing for God to displace everything but Himself from a share in the control of life—tradition, accepted social and business standards, preconceived ideas,

human ties which hinder us, our fears, our comfort, and everything else which has in the past dictated our actions. A business girl secures a change in the wages and working conditions of the rest of the staff, because she is no longer afraid to lose her job by stating the employees' case. A Dutch manufacturer invents a new form of incendiary bomb, for which he is offered a large sum of money. After meeting the Oxford Group at a house party in Switzerland, he is guided to destroy the formula. Though in great need of money, he obeys. Another man, retired and looking forward to more leisured days, sees that God needs his leisure. He sells his home, so that he may be free to go anywhere and do anything under God's orders. These are the men and women who start a revolution, because they are free from all ties except the will of God.

I have tried in previous chapters to sketch the outline of that thoroughgoing Christian life—surrendered, guided, shared and used by God—to which we are called. Nothing less will release the power of God into the life of our day. God needs men who are liberated from every other control but His.

We have hesitated at the cost. Revolutionary living means living out to-day the principles of the new world of to-morrow. We shall not wait for systems to be changed but shall let God take our life and hurl it at the fortifications of selfishness and wrong—this has always been costly. It is not simply that it is painful and difficult to us. It may involve deeply those we love—and there so many of us have

stopped short. The lost employment or diminishing business which means privation for them, the call to go ahead when they do not understand, and when God's way to the healing of a world seems to begin with wounds at home—these are the prices which are so hard to pay. They may have to be paid. God's way of life again and again turns out far better than our fears. It works in ways we never thought possible. But there are times when the conflict between a God-guided life and the present world means a cross, and someone broken and bleeding on it in obedience to a crucified Lord.

In the chapter of the Epistle to the Hebrews which speaks with confidence of the city whose builder and maker is God, there is also written the record of those who 'were stoned, sawn in two, and cut to pieces; they had to roam about in sheepskins and goatskins, forlorn, oppressed, ill-treated.' No man, called to fight for his country, regards it as a ground for refusing, that his wife may be widowed, his children orphaned, his business ruined. Nor does he consider their pleas the deciding authority. We are contending for far more than our country's victory.

In the end our own family life is lifted to a finer level and our children fired with a greater vision of God's purpose when we recognize and obey a claim higher than the claim of their comfort and safety.

We are not living any longer in that comfortable world of illusion, cushioned by prosperity, which made such talk of cost seem remote and unreal. Revolution knocks at the door. The Cross in our

lives is the only answer to the sickle and the hammer.

There is one other difference between our human attempts to reorganize society and God's way of re-creating it.

We can only reorganize as far as we can see. We have to wait until our slow human understanding has mastered some of the complex problems with which we are dealing. The process is too slow, too cautious and too uncertain, in a world where the forces of destruction can move so swiftly. We cannot afford to postpone action until our human eyes can see the shape of things to come. Yet there is nothing else for us to do, if human wisdom is all we have on which to rely.

Fortunately it is not. The plan of the new world is clear in the mind of God; and the immediate steps of our own obedience can become clear to us, if we will listen to God. If we have to go out 'not knowing whither'—unable to see how our obedience will work out—that is only the venture of faith which is inherent in Christian living. We shall see the shape of things to come as they actually take shape around the lives of surrendered men and women.

Our hope is in God's action. That hope is quickened by the fact that there is across the world to-day a growing army of men and women who are proving in their own lives that—

> *When man listens, God speaks;*
> *When man obeys God works.*

Healing-Habits.com is both humbled and honored to have the privilege of reprinting this classic work by Cecil Rose. This inspirational work, like many other great works was born out of the depths of the depression. Works like Dale Carnegie's How to Win Friends and Influence People, Florence Scovel Schinn's masterpiece The Game Of Life, Emmett Fox's Sermon On The mount, and Norman Vincent Peale's The Art Of Living. It is our great hope that with the rebirth of his classic that his words will heal the hearts and souls of all who read it. I will be eternally grateful to Cecil Rose for his impact on my life

Tuchy Palmieri President Healing-Habits

Made in the USA
Middletown, DE
20 April 2015